CW00953961

The Power of
The 9Fs

There were 251 standard '9Fs' built, but the class was only complete for a period of just over four years. The last to be built was No 92220 *Evening Star* in March 1960, and the first withdrawals came in May 1964. These included No 92177, which is shown on 6 August 1961 heading a down chemical train for the North East at Benningbrough, on the East Coast main line just north of York. The locomotive spent its entire career of just over six years allocated to Doncaster shed. *Gavin Morrison*

No 92215, allocated to Wakefield shed, makes a spectacular sight as it storms past Leeds Holbeck shed at the head of a Leeds Hunslet–Stanlow empty oil train. Originally it was a Western Region locomotive, which went new to Banbury shed where it stayed for four years before moving to Tyseley for three years, and finally Wakefield, from where it was withdrawn three months after this photograph was taken on 18 March 1967.
Gavin Morrison

The Power of
The 9Fs
Gavin Morrison

OPC

Oxford Publishing Co

Contents

Introduction	4
Construction Dates	7
Notable '9Fs'	8
The Franco-Crosti '9Fs'	16
On Shed	30
On the Southern Region	36
On the Somerset & Dorset	39
On the Western Region	47
On the London Midland Region	54
On the Great Central Main Line	75
On the Eastern Region	80
On the North Eastern Region	89
Working the Tyne Dock– Consett Iron-ore Trains	100
In Scotland	109
In Preservation	110

Bibliography

British Railways Standard Steam Locomotives, E. Talbot, Oxford Publishing Co

The Book of the BR Standards, Richard Derry, Irwell Press

Locomotives Illustrated No 5, Ian Allan Ltd

Title page:
No 92206 between duties at Eastleigh shed on 15 August 1961. *Gavin Morrison*

First published 2001

ISBN 0 86093 558 2

All rights reserved. No part of this book may be reproduced or transmitted in any form or by any means, electronic or mechanical, including photocopying, recording or by any information storage and retrieval system, without permission from the Publisher in writing.

© Ian Allan Publishing Ltd 2001

Published by Oxford Publishing Co

an imprint of Ian Allan Publishing Ltd, Hersham, Surrey KT12 4RG.
Printed by Ian Allan Printing Ltd, Hersham, Surrey KT12 4RG.

Code: 0110/B

Introduction

Class 9F, along with Class 3MT (77xxx) and the unique *Duke of Gloucester*, was one of the last BR standard classes to be introduced. With hindsight, the 251 members of the class must have represented the biggest waste of money ever spent on steam engines in the history of Britain's railways. The locomotives' construction cost rose by nearly 50% over the six-year period of building, from around £24,000 in 1954 to nearly £34,000 for the last of the class, *Evening Star*, in 1960. No 92210 had the shortest career of the class, lasting only 5¼ years, whilst No 92004 was the longest-lived, with just over 14 years. History now suggests that one of the finest classes ever to run on British Railways had the shortest careers. Given that BR's Modernisation Plan was presented in 1955, and that the first main-line diesels entered traffic from 1957 onwards, it is hard to understand why the BR Board thought it could ever justify the cost of 251 members of the '9F' class.

No 92000 emerged from Crewe Works in January 1954 at the start of its 11½-year career, and was posed for an official photograph alongside one of the last ex-LNWR 0-6-0 'Cauliflowers', which had just been withdrawn after over 70 years' service.

The class got off to a very bad start, being allocated to the Western Region at Newport for working the steel trains to Ebbw Vale. The first eight locomotives were definitely not appreciated by the Western crews, as apparently the steam brake was very slow to act after the locomotive had been standing, and the regulator was prone to sticking open — not exactly the features needed on the steeply-graded line up the valley to Ebbw Vale. On one occasion the sticking regulator resulted in No 92004 running into No 92005. The problem was solved by the fitting of a smaller valve, as used on the standard '4MT', but apparently the poor braking was never really resolved. The Western Region was not allocated any more of the class until No 92221 was transferred to Banbury in May 1958.

The appearance of the class varied mainly depending on the type of tender attached and whether or not they were fitted with single or double chimney. The exceptions were the 10 unsuccessful Franco-Crosti-boilered locomotives, which were all allocated initially to Wellingborough and worked mainly coal trains along the Midland main line. The anticipated savings in fuel costs were never achieved, and the crews disliked them due to drifting smoke from the chimney on the side of the boiler, which resulted in dirty cabs. All were eventually converted to conventional locomotives, No 92026 being the first, in September 1959.

There were several with special features, such as No 92079 with its headlight from the LMS 0-10-0 'Big Bertha' Lickey banker; those allocated to the Tyne Dock–Consett ore trains, with the Westinghouse pumps to operate the doors on the 56-ton ore wagons; and No 92250, unique in being fitted with a Giesl ejector, which it retained until withdrawn.

Large numbers were allocated to freight duties on the Midland main line, in the early years working chiefly south of Nottingham, whilst the Eastern Region received a large allocation at New England and Doncaster, these locomotives normally working the southern end of the line; the ex-Great Central depot at Annesley also had an allocation for working the famous Annesley–Woodford Halse 'windcutter' coal trains. The Western Region was allocated the last examples to be built, these working across the Region, although never allocated to the Newton Abbot division. The Scottish and Southern Regions never received any new '9Fs'.

Other than on the Western Region, the class appeared to be well liked and performed well, from the later 1950s being used on Summer Saturday extra passenger services. On such trains speeds of over 80mph were achieved on the Great Central main line, as well as on the East Coast main

Above:
A fine picture of No 92210 near Shepton Mallet on the Somerset & Dorset line, heading the Summer Saturdays-only 7.40am Bradford–Bournemouth express on 21 July 1962. The locomotive was in service for only 5¼ years — probably the shortest career of any BR standard locomotive — and during this period it was transferred seven times, ending its days at Newport Ebbw Junction in November 1964. *Ivo Peters*

line, where No 92184 was recorded as reaching 90mph down Stoke Bank on the up 14-coach 'Heart of Midlothian' on 16 August 1958. Apparently the '9F' gained 14 minutes (excluding delays) between Grantham and King's Cross, the schedule obviously being timed for an 'A1' or 'A4' Pacific. Records also exist of '9Fs' working the 'South Yorkshireman' and 'Master Cutler' expresses on the Great Central. It is also worth mentioning that, contrary to the Western Region's initial reaction to the class, Cardiff Canton used to employ No 92220 *Evening Star* on the up 'Red Dragon' express to Paddington along with its allocation of 'Britannias'. Apparently the authorities discouraged the use of '9Fs' on express workings, as no doubt the maintenance costs that resulted from the 5ft-diameter driving wheels' revolving at 8½ times per second (at 90mph) could be high. The log of the up 'Heart of Midlothian' trip of 16 August 1958 appeared in the November issue of *Trains Illustrated*.

TABLE I

E.R. GRANTHAM–KINGS CROSS

Engine: Class "9" 2-10-0 No. 92184.
Load: 14 coaches, 462 tons tare, 485 tons gross.

Dist.		*Sched.*	*Actual*	*Speeds*
miles		*min.*	*m. s.*	*m.p.h.*
0.0	GRANTHAM ..	0	0 00	—
3.5	Great Ponton ..	—	7 43	41
5.4	*Stoke*	9½	10 28	46
8.4	Corby Glen ..	—	13 24	78
13.3	Little Bytham ..	—	17 01	86
16.9	ESSENDINE ..	18½	19 26	90
20.7	Tallington	(†3)	22 08	86
26.0	*Werrington Junc.*	28½	26 14	76
29.1	PETERBOROUGH	33½	29 48	*25
30.5	*Fletton Junc.* ..	—	32 00	—
32.9	Yaxley..	—	34 48	—
36.1	Holme..	—	37 45	72
38.1	*Connington South*	—	39 27	70
42.0	Abbots Ripton ..	—	43 03	56
46.6	HUNTINGDON	52½	47 17	75
49.5	Offord	—	49 30	78
53.8	St. Neots	—	52 53	73
58.0	Tempsford	—	56 17	78
			p.w.s.	*29
61.4	Sandy	65½	59 16	—
68.5	Arlesey	(†2)	67 50	59
73.6	HITCHIN	79½	73 34	47
76.9	Stevenage	—	77 56	44/56
82.0	*Woolmer Green* ..	—	83 39	54/76
87.8	HATFIELD	94½	88 41	*61
		(†1)	*sigs.*	*30
92.8	Potters Bar ..	101½	94 10	—
		(†4)	*sigs.*	*24
103.0	FINSBURY PARK	115½	111 07	*30
			sigs.	*10
105.5	KINGS CROSS ..	120½	119 19	—

* Speed restriction. † Recovery time (min.).

It is noteworthy that the 10-coupled design had only been used for any size of class in this country on the War Department 2-10-0s (the wheel arrangement normally being associated with heavy freight haulage on railways elsewhere in the world), none of which would have been driven at 80-90mph, which speaks highly of the stability of the riding qualities of the Class 9Fs.

The class were a great success on the Tyne Dock–Consett ore trains, often acting as bankers, and also on the then well-known duties on the Shotton steel trains.

Possibly the biggest surprise of all during the class's short career came when the type was tested for passenger duties over the Somerset & Dorset line on 29 March 1960, when No 92204 easily hauled a 10-coach train plus van, unaided, in terrible weather conditions over the route's 1-in-50 gradients. Such ability was a major advantage on this line, where virtually all trains other than locals and freights were double-headed, leading to a shortage of crews and locomotives on summer weekends; the allocation for the summer months of four of the class solved such problems. This continued for the next few years until the through traffic was diverted away from the line in 1963, and *Evening Star* was chosen to haul the last 'Pines Express' workings over the route.

After this it was all downhill for the class: large numbers were withdrawn from the Western and Eastern Regions, and others were transferred to the North West — mainly to Birkenhead, Speke Junction, Carnforth and Carlisle Kingmoor — as the diesels took over.

The locomotives continued until there were only three of the class left by June 1968 at Carnforth. Externally they were usually very dirty, and their maintenance was kept to an absolute minimum, Curiously, however, most of the former 'Crosti' rebuilds survived into the last year of steam on British Railways.

Looking back on the few years of service that the class achieved, it must be said that the type was never really given the opportunity to show its real potential over a period of time. The '9Fs' were designed as freight locomotives, but, judging by their achievements on the Somerset & Dorset line as well as their other passenger exploits, they should perhaps have been classified '9MT'. One can only speculate as to what might have been, had they been allocated to the Highland main line or worked the double-headed expresses over the trans-Pennine Standedge route.

Fortunately, nine have passed into preservation, but so far only *Evening Star* has worked regularly over the main lines, with No 92203 making only a few outings. It is many years since *Evening Star* has been used, but there are plans for No 92212 to gain a main-line certificate.

As with other volumes in the 'Power' series, the object of this book is to produce a photographic record of the class, rather than illustrate or explain all the technical details, which are well covered in the books mentioned in the Bibliography.

Finally, my thanks go to the 84 different photographers whose pictures appear in this album, and without whom *The Power of The 9Fs* would probably never have been published.

Gavin Morrison
May 2001

Right:
An official photograph of No 92000 as it emerged from Crewe Works in January 1954, before being allocated to Newport (Ebbw Junction). *Ian Allan Library*

Construction Dates

Nos.	Annual programme	Built at	Building dates	Tender type	Region allocated
92000 92007	1953	Crewe	1/54-2/54	lG	WR
92008-92009	”	”	3/54	lG	LMR
920l0-92014	”	”	4/54-5/54	lF	ER
92015-92019	”	”	9/54-10/54	1C	LMR
92020-92029	”	”	5/55-7/55	lB	LMR
92030-92044	1954	”	11/54-1/55	lF	ER
92045-92059	”	”	2/55 10/55	lC	LMR
92060-92066	”	”	11/55-12/55	1B	NER
92067-92076	”	”	12/55 3/56	1F	ER
92077-92086	”	”	3/56-6/56	1C	LMR
92087-92096	”		8/56-4/57	lF	ER
92097-92099	1956	”	6/56-7/56	1B	NER
92100-92139	”	”	8-56-7/57	lC	LMR
92140-92149	”	”	7/57-10/57	1F	ER
92150-92164	”	”	10/57-4/58	lC	LMR
92165-92167	”	”	4/58-6/S8	1K	LMR
92168-92177	”	”	12/57-3/58	1F	ER
92178-92202	”	Swindon	9/57-12/58	1F	ER
92203-92220	1957	”	4/59-3/60	1G	WR
92221-922S0	”	Crewe	5/58-12/58	1G	WR

Total: 251

Below:
No 92000 was new from Crewe Works in January 1954.
It is seen here inside the erecting shop, with the boiler
mounted on the frame. *Ian Allan Library*

Above:
All members of the class from No 92178 onwards were built with a double chimney and blastpipe. This was after No 92178 was modified in 1957, although there was reportedly little difference in performance between the single- and double-chimney locomotives. Of the locomotives built with a single chimney, only Nos 92000, 92001, 92002, 92005 and 92006 were converted. No 92000 is shown in modified condition at Eastleigh shed on 4 August 1962, at which time it was allocated to Tyseley. *Gavin Morrison*

Below:
No 92079 went new to Toton in April 1956, but only stayed one month before moving to Bromsgrove to replace 0-10-0 No 58100, known as 'Big Bertha', on banking duties on the Lickey Incline. The '9F' was fitted with the headlight from 'Big Bertha', to help with 'buffering up' at night, and remained at Bromsgrove until October 1963, when it moved to Birkenhead, from where it was withdrawn in November 1967. It is pictured on 7 July 1956 at the Bromsgrove coaling stage for the bankers, along with various ex-LMS 'Jinty' 0-6-0Ts. *Gavin Morrison*

Left:
No 92079 gives banking assistance to a 10-coach train just outside Bromsgrove station on the 1-in-37 climb up the Lickey Incline on 7 July 1956. *Gavin Morrison*

Below:
Another banking duty on a passenger train is nearly complete as the fireman looks out from No 92079 as the summit of the Lickey Incline comes into view at Blackwell on 29 June 1957. *Gavin Morrison*

Right:
Ten members of the class —
Nos 92060-6 and 92097-9 — were
fitted with air pumps for operating the
hopper doors on the Tyne Dock–
Consett ore trains. The pumps can be
clearly seen on No 92097 at Consett
shed on 7 April 1957.
Gavin Morrison

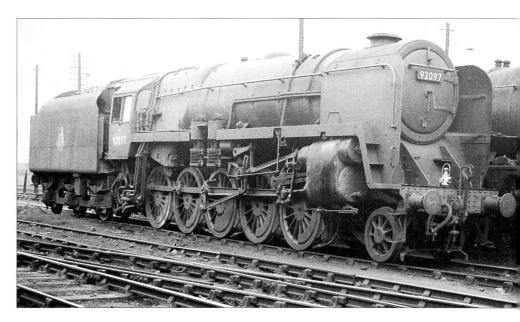

Centre right:
No 92178 was the first of the
Swindon-built '9Fs', and is seen in the
works yard on 15 September 1957
before entering traffic at New
England. Also the first to be fitted
with a double chimney, it completed
barely eight years in service.
Ian Allan Library

Below:
No 92178 was selected for trials
between Reading and Stoke Gifford in
early 1958, possibly because it was the
first of the class to be fitted with a
double chimney. The rest of the class
built after 1958 had a double chimney
and blastpipe, but it is said that in
traffic was little difference
between the single- and double-
chimney locomotives. The picture
shows No 92178, minus smoke
deflectors, approaching Winterbourne
with 14 coaches, including the
Western Region Dynamometer Car,
on 29 January 1958. *Ivo Peters*

Above:
Three members of the class, Nos 92165-7, were fitted with the American Berkley design of mechanical stoker. They emerged from Crewe Works in April and May 1958, and were allocated to Saltley shed. They were used mainly on Water Orton to Carlisle freights over the Settle– Carlisle line, with the Saltley crews working throughout. Specially-crushed coal had to be used.

At Kingmoor shed on 20 May 1961, No 92165 looks as if it has been repainted at the front after a minor mishap. The locomotive lasted until March 1968, being withdrawn from Speke Junction. *Gavin Morrison*

Left:
No 92166 alongside 'Britannia' No 70044 *Earl Haig* at Leeds Holbeck shed on 28 August 1961. The '9F' went to the Rugby testing plant during August 1958, as well as having a spell on the Western Region at Cardiff Canton and Newport (Ebbw Junction) in 1959. It was withdrawn from Birkenhead in November 1967. The mechanical stokers were removed after a few years.

Above:
No 92167 was the last of the trio to be withdrawn from Carnforth in June 1968. It is seen at Farnley Junction shed, Leeds, on 16 September 1966, while allocated to Birkenhead; Farnley Junction shed closed later that year. *Gavin Morrison*

Above:
No 92250 was the last steam engine to be built at Crewe Works, and was completed in December 1958. It was fitted with a Giesl Oblong Ejector, to try and improve coal consumption with normal grades of coal, and to allow lower grades of coal to be used. Savings were achieved, but, as steam traction was already in decline on British Railways, no further members of the class were modified. It spent its entire working career of seven years on the Western Region, and retained the Giesl ejector until withdrawn from Gloucester Horton Road in December 1965. *D. P. Williams*

Left:
A picture of No 92250 taken while the locomotive was allocated to Southall (note the 81C shedplate), between November 1963 and June 1964. *Ian Allan Library*

Below:
No 92250 heads an up freight through Shipton on 17 April 1965. *P. H. Wells*

This page:
No 92220 *Evening Star* was the last steam engine to be built at Swindon and for British Railways, being turned out by Swindon in March 1960. Painted in BR lined green livery, it was the only member of the class to be other than in plain black, and also had a copper-capped chimney. It duly entered service at Cardiff Canton, and was soon in use on the 'Red Dragon' express in the summer months. It was also used on the Somerset & Dorset, hauling the last 'Pines Express' on the Bath–Bournemouth route. Its career lasted only five years, before it was handed over to the National Railway Museum at York. These three pictures show the locomotive on Sunday 3 June 1962 at its then home shed of Cardiff Canton. *Gavin Morrison*

The Franco-Crosti '9Fs'

The Franco-Crosti-boilered '9Fs' were built at Crewe as Batch No E488 between May and July 1955. It was originally claimed that these boilers would reduce coal consumption by around 19%, and, as the railways had been ordered by the Government around this period to reduce coal consumption by 10,000 tons per week, it was obviously an experiment worth trying. The experiment was not a success, however, and from September 1959 onwards they were converted to conventional locomotives. They were classified only as '8Fs', as they had a smaller boiler than the other members of the class, and were not fitted with standard smoke-deflectors. As it turned out, they were among the last of the class to survive, all except No 92028 lasting almost to the end of steam on the London Midland Region at Birkenhead shed.

Above:
One of the locomotives under construction in Crewe Works, clearly showing the pre-heater drum under the boiler. *Ian Allan Library*

Left:
The front of No 92024 in Crewe Works when new, showing the pre-heater between the frames and the two access doors. *Ian Allan Library*

Right:
A view of No 92020 when new at Crewe in June 1955.
This clearly shows the chimney and the main pipe for the
exhaust steam from the right-hand cylinder. The normal
chimney was only used during lighting-up. *G. Wheeler*

Above:
In converted form No 92020 works a trans-Pennine freight
past Bradley Junction (east of Huddersfield), heading for
Lancashire. The locomotive was allocated for Birkenhead
and was frequently seen in the area, usually on Stanlow oil
trains. This was the site of Bradley station which closed in
1950; the two lines on the right have been lifted for many
years. The Bradley curve to the Lancashire & Yorkshire
main line can be seen in the background, to the left of the
signalbox; taken out of use in 1987, this link was reinstated
in 2000. *Gavin Morrison*

Left:
No 92020 at the end of its days, awaiting the scrapman's torch at Newport in 1968. *C. Gwilliam*

Right:
When only five months old, No 92021 heads up the Midland main line near Elstree with a coal train on 1 October 1955. This view clearly shows the exhaust leaving the chimney at the side of the boiler. *K. L. Cook*

Left:
Following complaints from crews about exhaust obstructing forward vision, Nos 92020-9 were fitted with a smoke-deflector around the chimney. No 92021 has just had a visit to Crewe Works and is shown on Crewe South shed on 12 October 1958. *A. W. Martin*

Left:
In terrible external condition, No 92021 had only another three months of service left when photographed plodding up the hill to Blea Moor on the Settle–Carlisle line at Ribblehead station on 5 August 1967. The quarry can just be seen on the right of the picture. Note the locomotive is now running with a BR1- or BR1A-type tender.
Gavin Morrison

Right:
No 92022 in original condition at its home shed of Wellingborough (15A) on 5 August 1955. *Gavin Morrison*

Right:
Another view of No 92022, again on Wellingborough shed but now with smoke-deflector, on 18 February 1962. By this time it was the only remaining 'Crosti' still to be converted to standard steaming, this work being completed by July 1962. *P. H. Wells*

Left:
A lucky picture at the north end of Hellifield station showing Standard '9F' No 92130 in the up loop being overtaken by No 92022 on 4 July 1964, one month after the latter had been transferred to Carlisle Kingmoor shed; it is heading an up van train.
Gavin Morrison

Below:
No 92022 has now lost its front numberplate. By this date — 8 July 1967 — it was allocated to Birkenhead, and is seen working a Hunslet–Stanlow oil train, which was a regular duty for these locomotives in their last years of service. It is passing Linthwaite, about halfway up the seven-mile climb at 1 in 105 from Huddersfield to Marsden.
Gavin Morrison

Right:
A close-up of the smoke-deflector fitted around the chimney of No 92023, seen on Leeds Holbeck shed on 14 December 1958.
C. Sheard

Below:
No 92023, again at Holbeck shed but this time in its final form, awaiting attention on the ash-pits on 24 March 1963. *Gavin Morrison*

Above:
An official works photograph of No 92024 taken at Crewe Works in June 1955 before the locomotive entered traffic. *British Railways*

Two pictures of the same train taken on the same day — 3 August 1957 — by different photographers. It must have been a very rare working for one of the Crosti-boilered locomotives to haul a Summer Saturdays-only extra from the East Coast (probably Scarborough).

Left:
With plenty of exhaust, No 92024 takes the line towards Church Fenton at Challoners Whin Junction, south of York. The 15A (Wellingborough) shedplate is just discernible. *P. B. Walker*

Below:
The same train about 15 miles further south, passing Pontefract as it heads towards Sheffield. *P. Cookson*

Above:
No 92024 produces a fine exhaust as it passes Bradley Junction (east of Huddersfield) on what was then the up fast line, as it starts the long climb over the Pennines to Diggle at the head of a Hunslet–Stanlow oil train on 29 September 1967.
Gavin Morrison

Right:
No 92025 in original condition at Wellingborough shed in 1958.
Ian Allan Library

Above:
No 92025 had apparently failed at Armathwaite whilst heading this up freight along the Settle–Carlisle line. By the date of the photograph — 3 June 1967 — it was a Birkenhead locomotive, and had only another five months left in service. *D. Cross*

Below left:
A couple of former 'Crostis': No 92025 stands at its home shed of Speke Junction together with Carlisle Kingmoor-allocated No 92021 and a Stanier Mogul on 26 May 1966. *I. G. Holt*

Below right:
No 92026 blackens the area surrounding Harlington station as it heads an up mineral train along the Midland main line during 1959. This was the first 'Crosti' to be converted to a conventional locomotive during September 1959. *M. S. Welch*

Above:
A view of No 92026 heading west along the Chester–Shrewsbury main line with a mixed freight at Llangollen Junction on 4 March 1967. The line to Llangollen and beyond can be seen in the background. *Gavin Morrison*

Right:
This picture was taken on 18 October 1967 and shows No 92026 on what was then one of the few steam workings left across the Pennines over the Standedge route. It is passing Gledholt Junction (just west of Huddersfield) on a Hunslet–Stanlow oil train. The locomotive had only a few weeks left in service, being withdrawn in November when Birkenhead shed closed to steam. *Gavin Morrison*

Left:
No 92027 in its original condition in the yard outside the shed at Wellingborough prior to 1959, when conversions started. *J. Davenport*

Left:
On 6 January 1964 No 92027 is again seen on Wellingborough shed, prior to being transferred to Kettering later in the month. Notice the 15B shedplate, Wellingborough having changed its code from 15A the previous September. *R. Wildsmith*

Right:
Smoke drifts gently out of the chimney of No 92028 as it awaits its next duty at Toton shed on 25 March 1956. This locomotive was the first of the Crosti-boilered locomotives to be withdrawn, in October 1966, and was one of only two (the other being No 92027) not to finish its working days allocated to Birkenhead.
J. Buckingham

Above:
Not long after being converted, No 92028 hurries an up freight along the main line past Marley Junction between Keighley and Bingley on 11 June 1960, when this section of line was still quadruple-track.
Gavin Morrison

Right:
No 92028 stands at Holbeck shed, Leeds, on 14 September 1963. The 2E shed code painted on the smokebox shows that, by the date of this photograph, the locomotive was allocated to Saltley, which shed had adopted this code earlier in the month but is best remembered as 21A.
Gavin Morrison

Left:
No 92029 was priming very badly as it passed Bedford with an up freight on 29 June 1957. *S. Creer*

Below:
No 92029 paid a visit to Bletchley in 1958. This view in the yard clearly shows the smoke-deflector, which appears to have the name 'Trembler' chalked on it. *P. Ransome-Wallis*

Above:
A rare visitor to Huddersfield Hillhouse shed in 1960, No 92029 had obviously just emerged from a visit to Crewe Works, at which time it was probably converted, when photographed on 15 August that year. *Gavin Morrison*

Below:
No 92029, by now allocated to Saltley shed in Birmingham, stands at Barnwood shed, Gloucester, in 1962.
N. E. Preedy

Right:
No 92234 at rest at its home shed of Banbury on 1 July 1966, before working a southbound freight later in the day. Except for its last years of service, No 92234 was allocated [exclusively] to Western Region sheds. Inside the shed can be seen No 92113, with 'Birkenhead' on the buffer-beam. *Ian Allan Library*

Below:
No 92100 at Holbeck shed, ready to leave after taking water. Apart from its final two years of service, it spent all its time allocated to sheds along the Midland main line. This picture was taken on 12 November 1961, when it was a Westhouses engine. *Gavin Morrison*

Right:
The caption on the back of the photograph says this picture of No 92087 was taken at Tyseley, and it is undated. It looks more like a shot taken in a works after the locomotive had been overhauled and was ready to re-enter service. Nevertheless a fine picture showing the BR Type 1F tender. *Ian Allan Library*

Left:
In terrible external condition, rebuilt 'Crosti' No 92021 of Birkenhead awaits servicing on the ash pits at Speke Junction shed on 26 May 1959. *I. G. Holt*

Below:
Unfortunately there are no details of this fine shed scene, but it was probably taken on Doncaster or New England shed between 1958 and 1963, when No 92191 was a Doncaster engine. Gresley 'O2' No 63942 stands alongside. *Ian Allan Library*

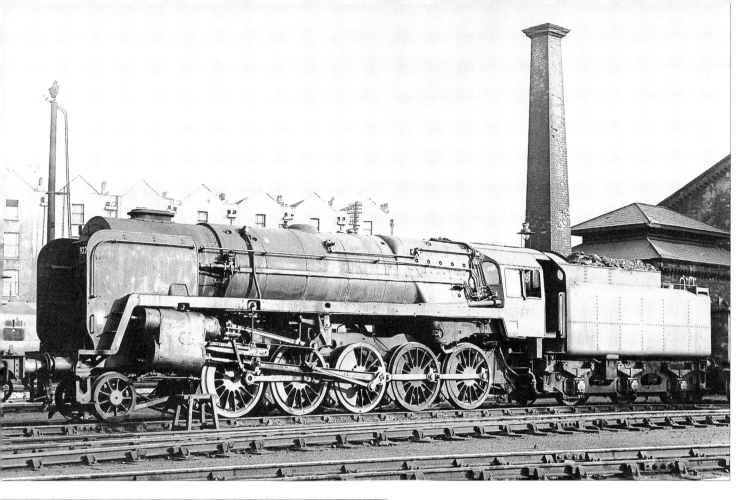

Above:
No 92248 was apparently 'dead' when photographed at its home shed of Bristol Barrow Road during September 1963. The locomotive was in service for only 6½ years, being withdrawn in June 1965 from Cardiff East Dock.
D. J. Wall

Left:
An atmospheric scene taken in one of the roundhouses at Leeds Holbeck shed, showing double-chimney No 92234 and an unidentified single-chimney '9F'. Although undated, the picture would have been taken during 1967, when No 92234 was allocated to Birkenhead; the latter shed closed at the end of September that year.
Ian Allan Library

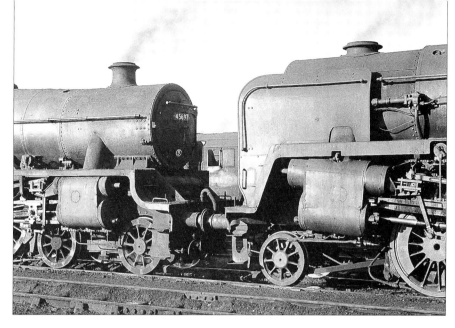

Right:
A fine study of front ends at Carlisle Kingmoor shed on 6 August 1966. Holbeck 'Jubilee' No 45697 *Achilles* is on the left and '9F' No 92080 on the right; the latter had only recently been transferred to Kingmoor when the photograph was taken.
A. R. Thompson

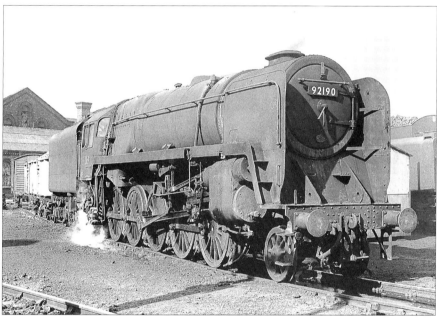

Left:
No 92190 at Leeds Holbeck shed on 4 October 1963. During its brief career of 7½ years this locomotive was allocated to many sheds — some not normally associated with '9Fs', such as Mexborough, Sheffield Darnall, Frodingham, Langwith and Colwick. At the date of this picture it was based at Colwick, which made it an unusual visitor to Leeds Holbeck.
Gavin Morrison

Right:
No 92239 was one of the five '9Fs' which were allocated to the Southern Region at Eastleigh. It is seen here on shed on 22 April 1962.
Gavin Morrison

Above:
It was not until 1961 that the Southern Region was allocated '9Fs', three being transfered in January followed by a further two in August; they were used on the 1,200-ton oil trains from Fawley to Toton. This picture shows No 92209 entering Bournemouth Central with a railtour which had just traversed the Hamworthy Triangle. On the right is 'Britannia' No 70020 *Mercury*, which had hauled the special from Waterloo to Salisbury and was booked to take the train back to Waterloo.
A. Richardson

Left:
No 92205 of Easteligh heads west out of Southampton with a very long pigeon special on 31 May 1963.
R. A. Panting

Right:
No 92002 ready to leave Basingstoke at the head of a Poole–Newcastle express, at the date of this picture — 20 August 1966 — it was allocated to Tyseley. *A. Swain*

Below:
A Fawley–Bromford Bridge petroleum train heads west through Salisbury station with Saltley's No 92136 in charge. The picture is undated. *P. Hutchinson*

Left:
An unusual working for Eastleigh-based No 92231 as it pauses at Southampton Central at the head of the 10.57am Salisbury–Portsmouth parcels, which it would work as far as Southampton Terminus, on 1 February 1961. This was usually a Standard '4' 2-6-0 working.
J. C. Haydon

Above:
Six months before being withdrawn, No 92220 *Evening Star* was on railtour duty with a 'Farewell to Steam' tour of the Southern Region. It is seen passing Axminster en route from Seaton to London Victoria on 20 September 1964.
J. C. Haydon

Left:
Franco-Crosti-boilered No 92028 on the Cliftonville spur between Hove and Preston Park, after a visit to Brighton Works for inspection on 9 September 1955. *J. H. W. Kent*

The '9F' class will always be associated with the Somerset & Dorset line, following the temporary transfer of a number to Bath in the early 1960s — the only time any members of the class were allocated purely for passenger duties.

Increased traffic in the summer months, particularly on Saturdays, always meant the S&D suffered severe problems with shortages of crews and locomotives, as all trains of over eight coaches had to be double-headed unless hauled by one of the line's famous '7F' 2-8-0s. Against this background, '9F' No 92204 was sent over from St Philip's Marsh shed at Bristol on 29 March 1960 to haul a 10-coach (plus one van) test train over the line unaided. In spite of terrible weather conditions, the trial was a complete success, resulting in Bath's receiving an allocation of four during the summer months. This became a regular transfer for the next two years, before main-line traffic was diverted away from the route.

'9Fs' allocated to the Somerset & Dorset at Bath shed (82F)

1960	92203, 92204, 92205, 92206
1961	92000, 92001, 92006, 92212
1962	92001, 92210, 92233, 92245 *
1963	92224, 92220
1964	92214, 92226 (for three weeks only)

* plus No 92220 which was drafted in to work the last 'Pines Express' via the Somerset & Dorset on 8 September.

Above:
In pouring rain, No 92204 climbing up the 1-in-50 bank out of Bath just before Devonshire Tunnel with the test train of van and 10 coaches on 29 March 1960. *Ivo Peters*

Below:
The weather conditions were obviously no better at Binegar than when the test train left Bath. No 92204 had just about another mile to go to Masbury Summit on the 8-mile climb from Radstock, mainly at 1 in 50. *Ivo Peters*

Above:
On the return journey from Bournemouth No 92204 paused for water at Evercreech Junction before tackling the 7-mile climb to Masbury Summit, again mainly at 1 in 50. During the few years that members of the class were used on the S&D, all were borrowed from the Western Region and thus all had double chimneys. *Ivo Peters*

Left:
Having just passed Bath Junction the 7.45am S.O. Bradford Forster Square-Bournemouth with No 92006 tackles the 1-in-50 climb to Devonshire Tunnel on 9 September 1961. *Gavin Morrison*

Left:
The summit of the steep climb out of Bath is just inside Coombe Down Tunnel. No 92245 bursts out of the very restricted bore at the head of the 7.45am Saturdays-only Bradford Forster Square–Bournemouth on 7 July 1962. *G. A. Richardson*

Below:
Another view of the 7.45am Bradford Forster Square–Bournemouth, again with No 92245, but this time crossing the viaduct at Midford (just south of the station) onto a double-track section on 28 July 1962.
Gavin Morrison

Right:
The up 'Pines Express' heads north over the easier gradients around Wallow on 28 July 1962, '9F' No 92210 being piloted by Standard '4MT' No 75009. The latter class replaced ex-LMS '2Ps' on the route after the summer services in 1961, although Nos 75071-3 spent nearly all their working lives allocated to Bath shed. *Gavin Morrison*

Left:
The 7.45am Bradford Forster Square–Bournemouth is well represented in this section. On 26 August 1961 it was hauled by No 92006, seen just south of Radstock at the start of the 8-mile climb to Masbury Summit. *Gavin Morrison*

Below left:
Another picture of the same train on the same day shows No 92006 leaving the short twin-bore tunnel at Chilcompton. The locomotive seems to be handling the train with the greatest of ease. *Gavin Morrison*

Right:
With only a few yards to go to Masbury Summit, No 92001 heads the 10-coach 9.35am Summer Saturdays-only Sheffield–Bournemouth on its journey to the South Coast on 12 August 1961. *Gavin Morrison*

Below:
The hard work is over for the fireman as No 92204 passes Masbury Summit at the head of a Bournemouth–Bradford Forster Square express on 20 August 1960. *I. Ross*

Left:
No 92212 bursts out of the twin-bore tunnel at Winsor Hill at the head of a Bristol–Bournemouth express on 26 August 1961.
Gavin Morrison

Left:
With only eight coaches behind the tender, No 92000 has a relatively easy time making the 1-in-50 climb at Winsor Hill Tunnel on its way to Masbury Summit with an up express on 12 August 1961. *Gavin Morrison*

Left:
No 92206 pauses at Shepton Mallet at the head of a four-coach Bristol–Bournemouth train in June 1960.
D. Cross

Right:
Former LMS '2P' No 40569 had only around another two weeks left in service when this picture was taken of it piloting No 92006 through Shepton Mallet with the up 'Pines Express' on 9 September 1961. The condition of the '2Ps' (externally, at least) was terrible, as in the late 1950s and early '60s they spent the winter months in store, emerging to act as pilots during the summer timetable. They were replaced by Standard '4MTs' (75xxx) following the end of the summer service in 1961. *Gavin Morrison*

Below:
No 92220 *Evening Star* was allocated to the line in the summer of 1963, although it appeared to spend most of its time on trains which could easily have been handled by less powerful types. This superb picture shows the '9F' against the water tower at the south end of Evercreech Junction station with the 1.10pm down train from Bath on 12 September 1963. *Ivo Peters*

Left:
It would appear that (during 1961, at least) the up 'Pines Express' received assistance from an ex-LMS '2P' between Evercreech Junction and Bath. Piloting No 92006, No 40634 pulls away from Evercreech Junction at the start of the climb to Masbury Summit on 12 August 1961.
Gavin Morrison

Right:
No 92245, with safety valves just lifting, passes through the wide cutting two miles north of Wincanton near the summit of the climb from Cole at the head of the Summer Saturdays-only 7.45am Bradford Forster Square–Bournemouth on 30 June 1962. *D. Cross*

Left:
No 92001 takes the spur connecting Templecombe Lower Junction, on the Somerset & Dorset line, with Templecombe station, on the London & South Western main line; it will reverse back to the junction before continuing its journey to Bournemouth on the track on the right of the picture. The shed was situated just behind the photographer, on the right. The picture is dated 7 July 1961. *M. J. Fox*

Right:
Tyseley-allocated No 92204 waits for the signals at Reading as 'Grange' class 4-6-0 No 6879 *Overton Grange* (the last of the class to be built) approaches with the 10.29am Reading–Woodford empties on 10 October 1964.
G. T. Robinson

Above:
An empty-stock train for South Wales coasts through Patchway with Newport Ebbw Junction's No 92209 in charge on 10 August 1963. *D. J. Wall*

Left:
No 92004 passes through Sonning Cutting on the down slow, with what looks like a train of scrap metal on 22 March 1964. The locomotive was allocated to Bristol Barrow Road at this time. *J. H. Patience*

Below:
When only a few weeks old and allocated to Bristol St Philip's Marsh shed, No 92207 arrives at Newport at the head of the 9.20am Swansea–Brockenhurst express on 27 June 1959. *J. Hodge*

Left:
No 92006 passing through Bridgend with a (very) light freight on 7 July 1962. This was one of the members of the class which was built with a single chimney and rebuilt with a double one. The few locomotives that received this modification seem to have been drafted into use on passenger duties on the Somerset & Dorset line in the early 1960s.
S. Rickard

Above:
A fine study of No 92204 as it prepares to leave Stratford-on-Avon with an engineers' train on 24 August 1963. The locomotive was allocated to Banbury at the time. *G. England*

Right:
The white exhaust from No 92227 stands out against the stormy black sky as it climbs out of Yate with a Saltney–Stoke Gifford freight on 24 July 1965. The train is on the line which runs off the former Midland route at Yate and joins the Western main line at Westerleigh West Junction. *C. D. Catt*

Right:
No 92244, allocated to Old Oak Common and (despite its external condition) only six months old, passes Stoke Gifford sidings with a coal train on 23 April 1959. *B. A. Poley*

Left:
An undated view of Saltley's
No 92137 hurrying along the former
Midland Railway Birmingham–Bristol
main line near Stonehouse.
P. Bridgman

Right:
No 92208, allocated to Cardiff East
Dock shed, passes Lansdown Junction,
Cheltenham, with a Washwood
Heath–Westerleigh freight on 27 July
1963. *S. Creer*

Below:
Saltley-allocated No 92151 races south
through Ashchurch with a freight for
the Bristol area, whilst in the
background a passenger train is ready
to leave for Evesham and possibly
Birmingham, the two lines coming
together again at Barnt Green. The
scene was recorded on 12 August
1961. *J. Robertson*

Above:
Bromsgrove and the Lickey Incline were transferred to the Western Region in early 1958. This picture shows No 92155 as it storms out of the loop at Bromsgrove and through the station before tackling the 1-in-37 ascent on 31 May 1963. No doubt there were two or three bankers at the rear of this long train. *D. Cape*

Right:
A very powerful picture of No 92155 near Berkley Road with the 2.55pm Leamington–Stoke Gifford freight on 22 August 1964. *G. T. Robinson*

Above:
An unusual train for No 92207, seen passing Solihull station with the 3.30pm Oxford–Birmingham on 27 August 1960. The express headcode hardly seems appropriate for the coaches. *M. Mensing*

Left:
No 92223, when nine months old and allocated to Banbury, approaches Acocks Green (on the Leamington–Birmingham main line) with a freight on 12 March 1959. This was the first '9F' to be withdrawn, in February 1964, but was reinstated and lasted almost to the end of BR steam, surviving at Carlisle Kingmoor until April 1968. *M. Mensing*

Above:
A very dirty Saltley '9F', No 92152, heads past Tyseley station, Birmingham, at the head of an up semi-fitted freight on 29 August 1959. *M. Mensing*

Below:
At the head of a long freight, No 92249 pauses to take water at Yeovil Pen Mill, possibly during the four-month period in 1960 when it was allocated to Plymouth Laira. *F. Church*

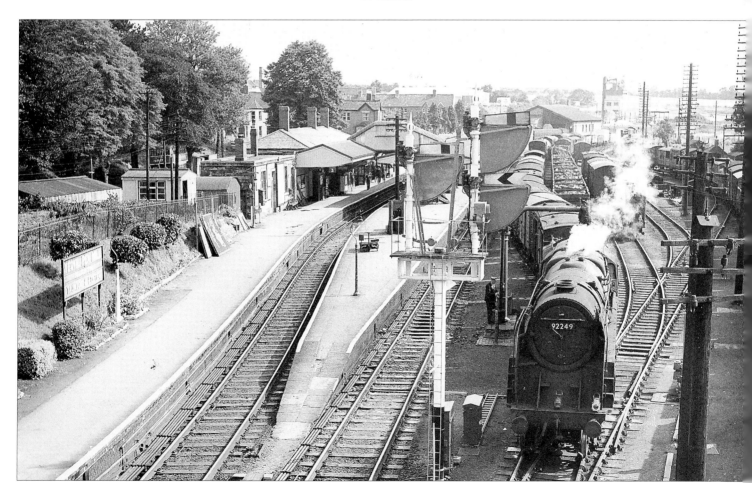

Left:
Between March 1954 and May 1958 the London Midland Region was allocated 100 new '9Fs'. Wellingborough received the first on the Region, and eventually had an allocation of around 40, including those with Franco-Crosti boilers; Toton was the next recipient, in September 1955, followed by Saltley, in April 1957.

This fine picture shows No 92102, which spent seven of its nine years' service at either Toton or Leicester, passing through Kenton c1959 with a train of then-modern hopper wagons. *D. Cross*

Above:
When only 10 months old and fitted with a smoke-deflector, Franco-Crosti-boilered No 92026 heads up the Midland main line with a coal train near Mill Hill on 20 April 1956. *A. R. Carpenter*

Left:
No 92009 was the second '9F' to arrive at Wellingborough, in March 1954, and was fitted with a 1G-type tender, which took 7 tons of coal and 5,000 gallons of water. Unfortunately there are no details available for this fine picture. *Ian Allan Library*

Right:
A well-known location on the Midland main line is the road bridge just to the north of Wellingborough station. No 92080, a Wellingborough locomotive at the time of the picture — 23 July 1960 — is shown heading north with a mixed freight. *A. Swain*

Left:
An unscheduled halt at Radlett for Franco-Crosti '9F' No 92029, to cut out a wagon with a 'hot box' which can be seen smoking, third from the engine. *P. Ransome-Wallis*

Left:
Wellingborough '9F' No 92077 passes BR/Sulzer Type 2 (later Class 24) No D5092 at Bedford station in October 1963. Whilst No 92077 put in only 12 years' service, the diesel fared very little better, being withdrawn after 15 years.
I. J. Hodson

Left:
Two Franco-Crosti '9Fs', Nos 92024 and 92021, head past Elstree, running light to Wellingborough on 16 July 1955. *P. J. Kelley*

Left:
No 92017 appears to be making good progress at the head of the 11.3am Brent–Wellingborough freight as it passes Mill Hill in 1954. The locomotive managed to put in over 13 years' service, not being withdrawn until December 1967, and spent half of that time based in the North West.
S. Creer

Right:
Kettering station does not seem to have altered much over the years. No 92123 of Wellingborough heads north with a coal train on 17 August 1957. The shed can just be seen on the left. *P. H. Wells*

Centre right:
No 92081 heads an up freight off the Corby line at Glendon Junction on 19 April 1961. The tracks on the left form the main line to Leicester. The locomotive spent most of its working life on the Midland division, with only a very short period at Annesley on the former Great Central, and finished its career with an 18-month spell at Newton Heath. *P. H. Wells*

Below:
No 92009 takes the Sheffield freight-line flyover past Trent station with a northbound iron-ore train on 19 April 1963. It will be noted that, compared to the picture on page 55, the locomotive has acquired a different tender. New in March 1954, No 92009 put in 14 years' service before being withdrawn from Carnforth — the second-longest term of active service for the class, exceeded only by No 92004 by two months. *C. P. Boocock*

Left:
On 5 April 1961, BR/Sulzer Type 4 (later Class 44) 'Peak' No D7 *Ingleborough* failed somewhere on the West Coast main line and had to be rescued by '9F' No 92122 of Leicester. The pair are seen after arrival at Euston station. *R. A. Panting*

Left:
No 92164, one of Saltley's '9Fs', slips as it restarts a heavy freight out of the yard at Nuneaton Abbey on 16 October 1965. It was transferred only once during its eight-year career, from Leicester to Saltley. *J. H. Cooper-Smith*

Above right:
A dirty No 92152 climbs towards Barnet Green with a Class 8 freight for the Bristol area on 22 August 1964. *F. A. Haynes*

Right:
Saltley-allocated No 92157 is on home territory as, assisted by a banker, it makes a determined effort to haul a heavy southbound coal up the steep climb to Camp Hill, Birmingham. The ensemble is passing St Andrews Junction on 19 August 1963. *C. P. Walker*

Left:
No 92122, by now allocated to Birkenhead, heads a load of empty wagons eastwards near Castle Donnington on 16 October 1965. *M. Mitchell*

Below:
Former 'Crosti' No 92021 is seen shunting spoil wagons in the yard at Wolverhampton Oxley on the afternoon of Sunday 17 October 1965. It appears to be just ex-works from Crewe — doubtless its last overhaul — and has been given a BR Type 1A tender, the 'Crosti' locomotives having originally been attached to Type 1Bs. *Gavin Morrison*

Right:
To mark the end of through passenger services between Paddington and Birkenhead, two specials were run on 4 March 1967. They were steam-hauled between Didcot and Chester by preserved 'Castles' Nos 4079 *Pendennis Castle* and 7029 *Clun Castle*. Between Chester and Birkenhead a couple of '9Fs' were used, both of which were well turned out for the occasion. No 92234 is seen approaching Hooton, where the train stopped for photographs to be taken. *Gavin Morrison*

Right:
The second special was hauled by No 92203 (now preserved and named *Black Prince*). The cleaners would seem to have run out of time, as the locomotive is clean but the tender appears untouched. This is another view at Hooton, where the train stopped. *Gavin Morrison*

Below:
Between August 1955 and May 1956 Bidston had an allocation of three '9Fs' (Nos 92045-7) for working the ore trains to Shotton. In the final years of steam Birkenhead took over the workings, and No 92111 is shown passing Heswall Hills on one such duty on 21 August 1967. *D. L. Percival*

Left:
Former 'Crosti' No 92026 (the first to be converted) slips as it leaves Chester with the Locomotive Club of Great Britain 'Severn and Dee' railtour on 26 February 1967. *I. G. Holt*

Left:
No 92126 takes the Chester avoiding line on the triangle to the west of Chester station with a tank train, possibly from Stanlow, on 7 May 1966. Chester No 6 signalbox (over the tracks) can be clearly seen, and behind it in the background are the buildings of the former Great Western shed. *I. S. Krause*

Below:
Birkenhead-allocated No 92111 climbs the 1-in-132 gradient away from Middlewich towards Sandbach at the head of the 18.06 Stanlow–Colwich tanks in July 1966. *Ian Allan Library*

Right:
The Summer Saturdays-only 10.10am Sheffield–Bangor is in the capable hands of Westhouses' No 92115 as it pulls away from Prestatyn on the last stage of its journey on 5 September 1959. *S. D. Wainwright*

Below:
Another '9F' from Westhouses shed, No 92116, approaches Llandudno Junction with a down Summer Saturday extra on 11 June 1960, overtaking 'Black Five' No 44691 on the down relief line. The line to Blaenau Ffestiniog can be seen on the right of the picture. *D. Cross*

Left:
On a dismal 3 November 1965 No 92139 of Saltley hurries down the bank through Doveholes with a special from Birmingham to Doncaster on the Stockport–Buxton line. *M. S. Welch*

Right:
No 92114 of Toton passes Manchester Exchange at the head of an empty wagon train and overtakes ex-Great Central Class O4 No 63700 in August 1960. *J. R. Carter*

Left:
A superb picture of No 92218 storming past Diggle station just before entering Standedge Tunnel with a down freight on 6 August 1966. *J. Clarke*

Left:
The flanges are probably squealing as No 92059 of Toton rounds the sharp curve off the Copy Pit line at Hall Royd Junction, Todmorden, and heads along the Calder Valley with a Summer Saturday extra from Blackpool to Yorkshire on 6 August 1960. Note the non-corridor stock. *R. S. Greenwood*

Right:
No 92118, by now a Carnforth locomotive, is piloted out of Skipton by BR/Sulzer Type 2 (later Class 25) No D5175 with a tank train from Heysham. The date is 30 September 1967, which was the weekend that steam finished in the North Eastern Region and that Leeds Holbeck and Low Moor sheds closed. Steam continued on a small scale after that date, with visits (mainly of '9Fs') from the London Midland Region. *Gavin Morrison*

Right:
Empty and loaded coal trains pass at the north end of Skipton station. No 92128 of Carnforth heads north on 29 March 1967. *Gavin Morrison*

Left:
Bell Busk station closed to passengers on 4 May 1959, but the signalbox remained open. Another of the many '9Fs' to end its days at Carnforth, No 92077, heads north with a mixed freight on 19 August 1967. *Gavin Morrison*

Right:
A superb picture of Saltley's mechanical-stoker '9F' No 92167 at the head of what was probably a Carlisle–Water Orton freight, approaching Bell Busk in the evening light on 16 May 1959. These workings of 226 miles were the longest in the country for a crew on a freight train, and the mechanical stokers were installed specifically for them. (They were removed in 1962.) No 92167 would be one of the last three of the class to be withdrawn from Carnforth at the end of BR steam. It is reported that it finished its days without its rear coupling rods, effectively running as a 2-8-2. *R. H. Short*

Left:
Regular passenger services to Hellifield finished on 6 September 1962, but the line remained open for freight. One such working was the Long Meg anhydrite trains, which towards the end of steam were worked by '9Fs'. No 92051, allocated to Carlisle Kingmoor, is seen a few miles south of Hellifield with an up train on 13 June 1967. Today the Blackburn–Hellifield line once again has a passenger service as far as Clitheroe, but there are no regular passenger workings between Clitheroe and Hellifield. However, it is still important as a diversionary route when the West Coast is closed, and for weekend specials, which are often steam-hauled. *Gavin Morrison*

Right:
No 92249 has had a change of tender from the BR Type 1G with which it entered service at Newport (Ebbw Junction) in December 1958. The locomotive had less than 10 years in service, being withdrawn in January 1968 from Speke Junction, from where it was often employed on the Long Meg anhydrite workings, as shown here as it pauses at Hellifield before setting off over the Settle–Carlisle line on 13 June 1967.
Gavin Morrison

Right:
Easy work for Kingmoor-allocated No 92058 as it drifts down the hill at Helwith Bridge, heading for Settle Junction on 30 September 1967. It was withdrawn just two months later.
Gavin Morrison

Below:
Former Franco-Crosti-boilered No 92021 was making very slow but steady progress towards Ribblehead and Blea Moor when photographed just north of Selside on a fine summer's afternoon on 5 August 1967. *Gavin Morrison*

Left:
No 92021's progress was such that there was plenty of time to photograph it again passing Dent. The picture was taken from the old signalbox — a location well used by photographers over the years.
Gavin Morrison

Right:
Another view of Dent, looking north out of the signalbox, shows No 92004 passing through the station with an up freight. The date being 8 December 1966, there is a little snow lying on the hills. No 92004 held the class record for length of service: it was new to Newport Ebbw Junction shed in January 1954 and, after seven transfers, ended its days at Carnforth in March 1968 — a life of 14 years and two months. *W. B. Alexander*

Below:
The fireman's hard work is over as No 92051 climbs the final 1-in-330 stretch to the summit at Ais Gill with a down freight on 5 August 1967. *Gavin Morrison*

Right:
On 25 May 1967 the Class 5 on the up 'Thames Clyde' relief failed further north, and a '9F' working an up Long Meg anhydrite train had to be commandeered. The train appears to be making good progress as it rounds the curve to Ais Gill summit at 1,169ft. *W. B. Alexander*

Below:
No 92009 spent 3½ years allocated to Carlisle Kingmoor and was often seen on the Long Meg Anhydrite trains; here it approaches Birkett Tunnel with an up working. Normally all the wagons would have been loaded, but not on this occasion. *W. J. V. Anderson*

Above:
No 92019 spent its last three years allocated to Carlisle Kingmoor shed. In this view the locomotive and its oil train have been put in the down loop at Grayrigg to let 'Britannia' No 70025 (minus its *Western Star* nameplates) pass by with a parcels train. *Ivo Peters*

Left:
No 92017 had only five months left in service when it was photographed at the head of an up heavy freight rounding the bend at Low Gill on 20 July 1967. *G. P. Cooper*

Left:
The Larbert–Oakley soda ash empties coast down Shap Bank past Greenholme in August 1967, headed by No 92076 during its last two years in service allocated to Carlisle Kingmoor shed.
G. T. Robinson

Right:
Allocated to Birkenhead for its final 4½ years, its days fitted with a mechanical stoker for working Carlisle–Water Orton freights are long over, No 92166 heads a down goods past Scout Green, banked by Fairburn 2-6-4T No 42210, in July 1965.
W. J. V. Anderson

Right:
This very heavy freight was apparently making extremely slow progress up Shap (15 minutes for the last 3 miles) past the Wells on 20 July 1967. The caption on the back of the print claims the '9F' was No 92214 but, as this was withdrawn from Severn Tunnel Junction almost two years earlier, cannot be correct. The banker was Standard '4MT' No 75026.
G. P. Cooper

Left:
No 92112 was in the perfect position at Hardendale Quarry for this fine passing shot with Stanier 'Black Five' No 44677 of Kingmoor heading north with an empty-stock working.
Ivo Peters

Right:
No 92205 is well away from its home shed of York as it passes Dentonholme North Junction at Carlisle with a Shap–Ravenscraig limestone train on 22 August 1964. This locomotive was allocated to Western, Southern and North Eastern Regions during its short, eight-year career. *D. C. Smith*

Left:
No 92093 passes its home shed of Carlisle Kingmoor with an up tank train on 4 February 1967. Notice the land on the left of the picture has been cleared in preparation for the construction of the new diesel shed.
Gavin Morrison

On the Great Central Main Line

Above:
A superb atmospheric picture of No 92068 climbing the
1 in 130 past New Basford just north of Nottingham with a
Woodford Halse–Annesley freight on 31 August 1963.

The station, which closed on 7 September 1964, can be
seen in the background, as well as the smoke from
Sherwood Rise Tunnel. *T. Bousted*

75

Above:
No 92030 emerges from the short tunnel to the south of Nottingham Victoria and passes the junction of the Grantham line as it heads south with an Annesley–Woodford Halse freight on 15 June 1963. *C. P. Walker*

Left:
No 92087 passes through Platform 7 at Nottingham Victoria as it hauls an Annesley–Woodford Halse freight. The exit signalbox can just be seen below the 'Way out' sign on the right of the picture. This fine station closed on 4 September 1967. *T. Bousted*

Right:
A fine night shot of No 92183 as it pauses at Nottingham Victoria in the early hours of 19 February 1965 at the head of a Marylebone–York parcels train. *J. Clarke*

Below:
No 92090 crosses the Great Central Viaduct as it approaches Nottingham Victoria with a Woodford Halse–Annesley freight on 15 June 1963. The line to Grantham can be seen in the foreground. *C. P. Walker*

Left:
No 92082 finds heading the 18.15 Nottingham–Rugby local easy work as it passes another train near Rushcliffe Halt on 19 May 1964. *M. Mitchell*

Right:
A very powerful picture as Nos 92067 and 92013 burst from beneath a bridge on the Great Central line after being 'looped' to allow a Cup Final special to pass on 25 May 1963. *C. P. Walker*

Left:
No 92090 hurries north past Charwelton on a coal train on 13 July 1959. The station, which closed on 4 March 1963, was situated on the other side of the bridge in the background. *Gavin Morrison*

Left:
'9Fs' were used on passenger workings over the route in the summer months during the late 1950s and early '60s. An unidentified locomotive is seen climbing away from Leicester at the head of the 8.5am Bournemouth Central–Leeds on 27 July 1963. *G. D. King*

Right:
No 92057 is working hard as it climbs Ashby Bank with an up stone train on 4 November 1961. *M. Mitchell*

Left:
Rushcliffe Halt can just be seen in the background through the bridge as No 92071 heads south with a coal train from Annesley to Woodford Halse on 16 July 1974. *T. Bousted*

Right:
In May 1954 March shed received five new '9Fs' (Nos 92010-92014) for use on the Great Eastern line via Cambridge to London. No 92010 heads a down freight past Broxbourne on 23 July 1955. *E. R. Wethersett*

Below:
When only four months old, No 92014 heads an up coal train near Trumpington (south of Cambridge) on 7 September 1954. Like No 92010 in the previous picture, No 92014 is attached to a Type 1F tender, which had capacity for 7 tons of coal and 5,625 gallons of water. *E. R. Wethersett*

Right:
Doncaster and New England (Peterborough) sheds received large allocations of '9Fs', and during the late 1950s and early '60s the type became the dominant form of motive power for freight at the southern end of the East Coast main line.
No 92187 is shown climbing away from King's Cross goods yard on a down freight on 27 April 1963. Built in February 1958, this locomotive had a career of only seven years, being withdrawn in February 1965.
G. T. Robinson

Left:
In the blizzard conditions that ended 1962 and continued on well into 1963, No 92142 of New England heads a down freight through the snow near Potters Bar on 28 December. This locomotive put in only 6½ years' service, all of it at New England shed. *Brian Stephenson*

Right:
Doncaster shed's No 92174 approaches Finsbury Park with 40 vacuum-fitted, 16-ton mineral wagons for King's Cross on 8 May 1958.
Ian Allan Library

Left:
No 92170 heads north with a short cement train, just south of Peterborough on 20 July 1961. This was another '9F' which had only 6½ years of service. *D. C. Ovenden*

Left:
During its time at New England, No 92035 is seen working hard as it hauls an up freight off the slow line through Sandy station.
Ian Allan Library

Above right:
By the date of this photograph (25 May 1963) the Uddingston–Cliffe cement was usually hauled by the Southern Region's BRCW Type 3 (Class 33) diesels, but '9F' No 92040, seen approaching Knebworth, had been drafted in to cover a failure. Note the chalked number 040 on the cabside. *Ian Allan Library*

Right:
No 92182 passes under one of several similar road bridges across the East Coast main line south of Stoke Summit at the head of an up coal train near Abbots Ripton on 18 July 1961. *D. C. Ovenden*

Above:
A fine picture showing No 92040 passing Huntingdon North with an up coal train on 23 July 1959. Note the locomotive is carrying larger cabside numbers than normal. *D. C. Ovenden*

Below:
An up coal train headed by New England's No 92041 leaves Peterborough and approaches Fletton Junction on 30 March 1955. *P. H. Wells*

Right:
New England's No 92187, with 12 coaches behind the tender, approaches Peterborough at the head of a down express on 25 July 1959. Around this time the '9Fs' were used on Summer Saturday reliefs on the East Coast main line, and speeds of up to 90mph were being recorded. It is said these exploits came to an end after a senior Eastern Region official, travelling up to King's Cross, went to congratulate the crew on regaining some lost time, thinking it was a Pacific on the train; much to his surprise he found a '9F' at the buffer stops. After that, 90mph running with '9Fs' was not encouraged. *D. C. Ovenden*

Left:
The main duty for the New England '9Fs' was working coal trains to and from London. No 92183 approaches the north end of Peterborough station with an up working during July 1961. *J. C. Baker*

Below:
New England's No 92141 rounds the curve at High Dyke before reaching the summit of the climb from Barkston, at the south end of Stoke Tunnel, on 2 August 1958. Cows are clearly visible in the cattle wagon at the front of the train. *Gavin Morrison*

Above:
On a fine summer's day in August 1958, New England's No 92179 passes High Dyke at the head of a down relief express. *T. G. Hepburn*

Below:
In terrible external condition, Doncaster's No 92177 heads up the slow line past Little Ponton to Stoke Summit on 1st September 1962. This locomotive was in the first batch of '9Fs' to be withdrawn, in May 1964. *Gavin Morrison*

Right:
When new in March 1958 No 92189 was allocated to Mexborough, and then had spells at Darnall, Doncaster, Frodingham, Doncaster (again), Colwick and Langworth, finally being withdrawn from Colwick in December 1965. This was quite unusual for the Eastern Region '9Fs', which generally were not reallocated very often, although No 92190 followed a similar pattern. Here No 92189 descends from Stoke Summit with an up freight, passing the site of Little Bytham station, which had closed to passengers on 15 June 1959. The picture is dated 25 August 1964, at which time the locomotive was allocated to Colwick. *P. H. Wells*

Below:
The 3.15pm Doncaster–London East Goods approaches Retford, headed by New England-allocated No 92141 on 2 August 1958. It will be noted that the author photographed this train at High Dyke (page 85). *R. J. Buckley*

Above:
The rebuilt Franco-Crosti locomotives were seldom seen on the East Coast main line. No 92020 approaches Doncaster station with a down goods from Decoy sidings on 30 September 1967. *J. Cooper-Smith*

Left:
At Langwith Junction in the early 1960s a member of the crew climbs aboard No 92038 on a train to High Marnham power station.
Ian Allan Library

Right:
No 92070 is well away from its home shed of Leicester as it heads up the East Coast main line at Chester Moor, just south of Chester-le-Street, at the head of a special van train on 29 August 1964. *I. S. Carr*

Below:
No 92137 of Saltley, Birmingham, negotiates the complex track layout at the north end of Newcastle Central, heading for Platform 10 with an up fitted freight on 13 April 1960. *I. S. Carr*

Left:
A coal train for Consett passes a colliery near Leadgate with one of the Tyne Dock '9Fs', No 92063, during November 1964. *W. J. V. Anderson*

Below left:
This fine view shows the track layout at South Pelow Junction as Tyne Dock '9F' No 92097 leaves for Consett with a loaded coal train in May 1964. *W. J. V. Anderson*

Above right:
No 92189 passes Dearness Valley with a down freight diverted via Bishop Auckland on Sunday 30 July 1961. The Waterhouse branch curves to the right, behind the train. *I. S. Carr*

Centre right:
Different traffic for Consett, this time an oil train, headed by another Tyne Dock '9F', No 92062. The train is seen pulling out of Bensham goods yard (near Gateshead), with the East Coast main line on the right, on 26 June 1964. *M. Dunnett*

Below:
New England-allocated No 92184 leaves York with an up express on 22 August 1959. The goods avoiding lines can be seen curving away to the left of the picture, and the roof of the south shed roundhouse is visible above the first and second coaches. *K. R. Pirt*

Left:
The same location as the last picture sees another New England '9F', No 92035, heading south with a cement train on 16 June 1963. *Gavin Morrison*

Right:
The Heysham–Tees Yard oil train, hauled by No 92077, one of Carnforth's '9Fs', is seen just inside the North Eastern Region at Cononley, a few miles south of Skipton, on 17 March 1967. *Gavin Morrison*

Right:
Freights pass at Pontefract Baghill, as No 92055 heads south towards Sheffield. The shed code on the '9F' is 15A, denoting its allocation to Wellingborough. *K. Field*

Left:
No 92048 of Birkenhead pulls out of Neville Hill yard towards Marsh Lane cutting and Leeds station with empty oil tanks for Stanlow from Hunslet on 29 April 1967. *Gavin Morrison*

Right:
With an up freight on 18 April 1967, Carlisle Kingmoor-allocated No 92223 passes Kildwick station, which had closed just over two years earlier, on 22 March 1965. *Gavin Morrison*

Left:
Another view of a Heysham–Tees Yard oil train, here headed by No 92212 of Carnforth is approaching Bingley on 17 March 1967.
L. A. Nixon

Centre left:
No 92093 was new to Doncaster in January 1957 but spent most of its days working on the Great Central. Its final 21 months before being withdrawn in September 1967 were at Kingmoor. The locomotive is seen here on 19 July 1967, about to leave Bradford Valley Road Goods on the 19.40 freight to Carlisle.
Gavin Morrison

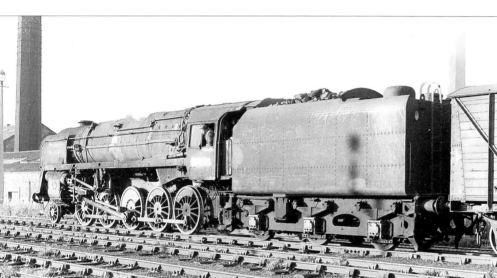

Below:
In terrible external condition, No 92109 of Birkenhead passes through Rodley cutting (north of Leeds) on the 12.55pm Stourton–Carlisle freight, including some ICI tanks, on 17 June 1967.
Gavin Morrison

Above:
A busy scene at Wortley Junction, Leeds, on 5 May 1961, viewed from the signalbox steps. No 92104 of Leicester, heading an up express freight from Carlisle, passes local Ivatt 2-6-0 No 43044, ready to leave the sidings after collecting wagons from the gas works, which had the unfortunate habit of blowing dirty smoke across the tracks and thus ruining photographs. *Gavin Morrison*

Below:
Another view at Wortley Junction sees No 92051 of Carlisle Kingmoor heading back home at the head of the 3.25pm Stourton–Carlisle freight on 16 August 1966. Holbeck High Level and Low Level stations, both of which closed on 7 July 1958, were located by the bridge in the background, which carried the Great Northern main line into Leeds Central. *Gavin Morrison*

Left:
Former Franco-Crosti '9F' No 92024 passes Holbeck shed, Leeds, with an empty Hunslet–Stanlow tank train on 14 April 1967. The viaduct in the background carried the old LNWR Manchester line, which the tanks will join at Thornhill Junction, Ravensthorpe. *Gavin Morrison*

Below:
A busy scene between Mirfield and Heaton Lodge Junction on 16 June 1967, with an up coal train heading west as a very heavy Stanlow–Hunslet oil train passes. Ex-LMS 'Black Five' No 45324 of Heaton Mersey shed, Stockport, pilots ex-mechanical-stoker '9F' No 92165, which would have another nine months in service at Birkenhead. *Gavin Morrison*

Right:
Rebuilt 'Crosti' No 92022 seems to be preparing for the climb to Marsden as it takes water at Huddersfield station before setting off and immediately entering the 684yd Springwood Tunnel on 8 July 1967. Prior to the Grouping, the massive warehouse in the background was owned jointly by the London & North Western and Lancashire & Yorkshire railways. It is still standing in the year 2001, but has not been used by the railway since 1970. *M. Dunnett*

Below:
By pure chance the author recorded the same train on the same day, shortly after the previous photograph was taken. No 92022, now well into its stride on the 1-in-105 climb up to Marsden, is shown passing Gledholt Junction. *Gavin Morrison*

Left:
Complete with brake vans at both ends and barrier wagons, No 92048 heads an up tank train past Mirfield shed on 16 June 1967 — three months before it was withdrawn from Birkenhead. The freight on the up slow on the right of the picture appears to be heading in the down direction, possibly to gain access to the marshalling yards at the east end of the station. *Gavin Morrison*

Left:
Its days on the Western Region, where it was allocated when new in September 1959, are long gone as No 92211 struggles past Milnsbridge *en route* to Marsden with a freight for Lancashire on 8 February 1967; its pace was such that there was no difficulty in obtaining further pictures before the train entered Standedge Tunnel. By this time the '9F' was allocated to the ex-Lancashire & Yorkshire shed at Wakefield, from where it would be withdrawn three months later. *Gavin Morrison*

Left:
Another picture of No 92211, still struggling up the bank to Marsden, and now running into thin fog as it nears the summit. *Gavin Morrison*

Above:
At 700ft above sea level, former Franco-Crosti-boilered No 92020 heads into the single-bore 'Nelson' tunnel through Standedge on 4 June 1966. The single-bore tunnels were closed from 31 October 1966, when the fast lines between Huddersfield and Diggle were taken out of use. *Gavin Morrison*

Right:
No 92054 pauses with a coal train in the up loop at Hebden Bridge to let the famous Heaton–Red Bank vans overtake. When this picture was taken on 23 July 1964, the locomotive had only recently been transferred to Speke Junction shed. The '9Fs' were not often seen on the Calder Valley line in 1964, 'WDs' and Stanier '8Fs' being the regular motive power for freight workings. *Gavin Morrison*

Ten '9Fs' were allocated to Tyne Dock for working the iron-ore trains to Consett; these were Nos 92060-6/97-9, all of which are featured in this section.

The '9Fs' replaced five 'O1' 2-8-0s which had been sent to the line in 1952. Each locomotive was fitted with two 10in Westinghouse air compressors mounted on the right-hand side, which maintained a pressure of 90psi when the wagons were loaded and also operated the wagon doors for discharging the ore at Consett. The first '9Fs' arrived new in November 1955 but were promptly transferred to Wellingborough to help out with the crisis caused by problems with the Franco-Crosti-boilered locomotives. They returned after six months, some

Above:
No 92066 stands under the loading bunkers at Tyne Dock prior to hauling the train to Consett on 18 March 1964.
Gavin Morrison

spending a short spell at Toton on the way back, and thereafter settled down to around 10 years' work on the steeply-graded line. Nos 92097-9 went direct to Tyne Dock when new and remained at that shed until withdrawn. Indeed, of the 10 dedicated locomotives, only No 92065 moved away, spending its last six months at Wakefield shed.

Above:
A close-up view of No 92066 prior to departure from Tyne Dock on 18 March 1964. *Gavin Morrison*

Right:
In May 1956 No 92097 storms up the 1-in-37 climb out of Tyne Dock with the help of 'Q6' 0-8-0 No 63373 at the rear. There is a lot of hard work in store for the crews, as the line rises by 900ft in the next 22 miles, with gradients as steep as 1 in 35. *J. R. P. Hunt*

Left:
No 92065 approaches Pontop Crossing as it nears journey's end with a train of empties on their way back from Consett to Tyne Dock on 14 August 1962. *I. S. Carr*

Right:
Another picture of a Tyne Dock departure: No 92062 heads the 11.10am on 13 March 1965. Another '9F' can be seen in the distance on an iron-ore train. *J. R. P. Hunt*

Left:
The guard on the Tyne Dock–Consett iron-ore train prepares to couple-up the banking engine — No 92099 — at South Pelaw on 27 May 1964. *M. Dunnett*

Left:
No 92060 passes between High Street (Gateshead) and King Edward Bridge Junction with a Tyne Dock–Consett ore train on Sunday 1 May 1966. It was not uncommon for trains to use this route on Saturday afternoons and Sundays, when the route via Washington was closed. *I. S. Carr*

Right:
A powerful picture of No 92064 storming out of South Pelaw with a loaded train for Consett on 14 October 1964. *J. R. P. Hunt*

Left:
The last steam-hauled iron-ore train from Tyne Dock to Consett ran on 19 November 1966. Locomotive No 92063 was cleaned for the occasion, and made a fine sight leaving South Pelaw. *V. Wake*

Below:
Having travelled via Birtley and High Street (Gateshead), a train of empties headed by No 92097 prepares to take the Boldon Colliery line as it returns to Tyne Dock via Pelaw on 23 July 1966. As already stated, this route was usually taken at night, on Saturday afternoons and on Sundays, when the direct line through West Boldon and Washington was normally closed. *I. S. Carr*

Right:
A loaded train with Nos 92063 and 92098 in charge catches the afternoon light as it climbs between Pelton and Beamish on 29 April 1964.
M. Dunnett

Right:
A loaded ore train of nine wagons passes Pelaw South Junction with Nos 92061 and 92062 in charge. The gradient here was 1 in 56, which steepened to 1 in 35 for a short stretch. The train has just left the Pontop and South Shields branch (on the left of the picture), along which it has travelled from Tyne Dock, and will continue its journey to the works over the Blackhill line. *C. H. Dean*

Right:
A busy scene at South Pelaw shows No 92064 restarting a loaded train, with another '9F' assisting in the rear. A 'Q6' 0-8-0 can be seen in the background, along with an English Electric Type 3 (Class 37) diesel.
V. Wake

Left:
No 92098 heads an empty train down the hill past Beamish signalbox. *V. Wake*

Right:
Another, more general view at Beamish sees No 92065 descending with empties for Tyne Dock in April 1964. *W. J. V. Anderson*

Left:
A loaded train climbing past Beamish with No 92064 in charge on 1 May 1966; an English Electric Type 4 (later Class 40) acting as a banker is just visible at the rear of the train. *V. Wake*

Right:
No 92061 bursts out of the short tunnel at Beamish as it climbs the 1-in-51 gradient, bound for Consett on 5 July 1966. *G. McLean*

Below:
Another view of No 92061, passing Beamish signalbox and the site of the station, which closed to passengers on 21 September 1953. This picture was taken in June 1964. *W. J. V. Anderson*

Left:
No 92099 is being banked by 'WD' No 90434 as it storms past Stanley with a loaded train on 18 March 1964. *Gavin Morrison*

Left:
'9Fs' Nos 92061 and 92062 climbing the 1-in-54 gradient between Stanley and Annfield Plain with a load of 787 tons gross. *C. H. Dean*

Left:
Journey's end for No 92066 as it arrives at the unloading hoppers on a wintry 18 March 1964. The Consett Iron Company was established in 1864, but, due to the excessive cost of operating the plant, the furnaces were allowed to cool for the last time in 1983. The scrap from the plant was taken away by train to Sheffield, the last running on 30 September 1983. *Gavin Morrison*

Right:
Pictures of '9Fs' in Scotland appear to be fairly rare; the Region never had any members of the class allocated, and it was not until the last years of BR steam, when Carlisle Kingmoor received an allocation, that they were seen north of the border. On 1 August 1964, during its 3½-year spell at Kingmoor, No 92249 descends Beattock Bank with an empty-stock working at the end of the Glasgow Fair Holiday. This locomotive had been new in December 1958 to the Western Region, but stayed only until October 1960 before moving to the London Midland Region, where it remained until withdrawn in July 1968.
P. Riley

Below:
A rare photograph of a Franco-Crosti '9F', No 92023, leaving Hurlford for Carlisle with a test train comprising Dynamometer Car No 3, mobile test units Nos 2 and 3 and a passenger brake van, on 18 October 1955. *W. A. C. Smith*

In Preservation

Happily, nine members of the class have survived into preservation. Of these, only one — No 92134 — is of the single-chimney type, all the others — Nos 92203/7/12/4/9/20/40/5 — being double-chimney locomotives. Apart from Nos 92240/5, built at Crewe, all the survivors were constructed at Swindon.

At the time of writing only two members of the class have worked on the main line in preservation, these being No 92203 and No 92220 *Evening Star*. No 92203 made only a handful of runs in the early 1970s, while *Evening Star* has not been out of the National Railway Museum for many years. Nos 92212 and 92240 are currently in use on preserved lines, and the others are in the course of restoration.

Right:
The Keighley & Worth Valley Railway was fortunate in being loaned *Evening Star* by the National Railway Museum in 1973; it arrived at Keighley on 4 June 1973 and was soon at work on the line. Towards the end of its stay it was allowed to work a special to Steamtown, Carnforth, on 31 May 1975, where it is seen in this picture alongside German '01' Pacific No 01-1104. *Gavin Morrison*

Above:
No 92203 is seen on one of its very few main-line outings, near Chandler's Ford on 13 May 1973, working one of the specials between Eastleigh and Romsey in connection with the Eastleigh Works open day. *R. Cover*

Right:
On the fine evening of 31 May 1975 the special made a superb sight heading south past Kettlebeck towards Settle Junction, on its return journey from Carnforth to the K&WVR. *Gavin Morrison*

Above:
Evening Star was back in action on 4 July 1976, when it worked to Scarborough from York. It is shown on the curve at Kirkham Abbey on the return journey to York. *Gavin Morrison*

Right:
On 20 May 1977 *Evening Star* was used to haul preserved GNR Ivatt Atlantic No 990 *Henry Oakley* to the Keighley & Worth Valley Railway, where it was to be returned to steam. After turning on Shipley triangle, *Evening Star* returned to Keighley to collect the National Railway Museum's Hughes 'Crab' No 42700, which had been on loan for several years, and take it back to York. On the outward journey, *Evening Star* emerges from Thackley Tunnel as the late John Bellwood, then in charge of the locomotives at the museum, has a quick look out of the cab to see that all is well. *Gavin Morrison*

Left:
Evening Star made several trips over the Settle–Carlisle line, one on a blustery, wet 13 May 1978, when it hauled the up 'Border Venturer'. It is seen crossing the old A66 road as it departs Appleby in fine style. *Gavin Morrison*

Left:
Working a northbound 'Cumbrian Mountain Express', *Evening Star* is making excellent progress near Horton-in-Ribblesdale with a heavy 13-coach train on 21 April 1984. Such a load would definitely have involved double-heading in the days of regular steam on the Settle–Carlisle line. *Gavin Morrison*

Left:
Evening Star has just taken water from a road tanker at Ribblehead station and is ready to leave with the up 'Cumbrian Mountain Express' on 23 April 1984. This was one of the few occasions when the train was allowed to reverse back over the viaduct to give a run-past for photographers. *Gavin Morrison*